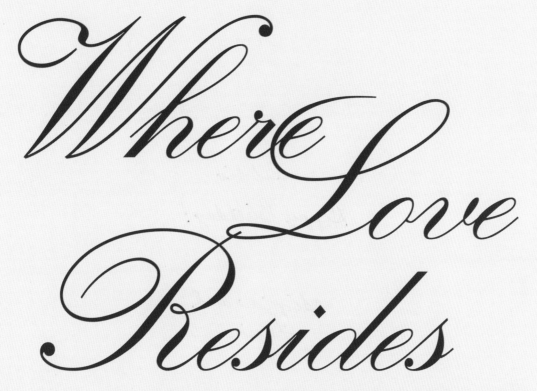

Where Love Resides

REFLECTIONS ON LOVE AND LIFE

That Patchwork Place

Credits

Excerpts from the book *How to Make an American Quilt* by Whitney Otto © 1991 by Whitney Otto. Reprinted by permission of Villard Books, a division of Random House, Inc.

How to Make an American Quilt Screenplay by Jane Anderson.

Excerpts from the film *How to Make an American Quilt* TM & © 1995 Universal City Studios, Inc. and Amblin Entertainment, Inc. All Rights Reserved. Licensed by MCA/Universal Merchandising, Inc.

Where Love Resides is a trademark of Universal City Studios, Inc. and Amblin Entertainment, Inc. All Rights Reserved.

COMPILATION TEAM	Greg Sharp
	Sharon Gilbert
	Kerry I. Hoffman
	Margaret Philip
	Alane Redon
CONTRIBUTING WRITERS	Kathy Hoggan
	Laura M. Reinstatler
	Ursula Reikes
COPY EDITORS	Liz McGehee
	Tina Cook
PROOFREADER	Melissa Riesland
DESIGN DIRECTOR	Judy Petry
TEXT AND COVER DESIGN	Barbara Schmitt
PRODUCTION ASSISTANTS	Claudia L'Heureux
	Brian Metz
ILLUSTRATOR	Laurel Strand
PHOTOGRAPHER	Brent Kane

For additional credits, see page 62.

That Patchwork Place, Inc.
PO Box 118, Bothell, WA 98041-0118 USA

MISSION STATEMENT

WE ARE DEDICATED TO PROVIDING QUALITY PRODUCTS AND SERVICES THAT INSPIRE CREATIVITY.

WE WORK TOGETHER TO ENRICH THE LIVES WE TOUCH.

That Patchwork Place is a financially responsible ESOP company.

Library of Congress Cataloging-in-Publication Data

Where love resides / compiled by That Patchwork Place.
    p. cm.
  ISBN 1-58477-145-8
    1. Patchwork—Patterns. 2. Quilting—Patterns.
3. How to make an American quilt (Motion picture) I. That Patchwork Place, Inc.
TT835.W49   1996
746.46—dc20
                                                    95-46917
                                                        CIP

Printed in Hong Kong
01 00 99 98 97 96   6 5 4 3 2 1

Young lovers seek perfection
Old lovers learn the art
of sewing shreds together,
and of seeing beauty in
a multiplicity of patches.

Contents

INTRODUCTION
Where Love Resides

Love, Life, and Quilts. For centuries, women have expressed their values through a creative blending of heart, home, and hands. Imagine a group of women around a quilting frame, young and old, with vastly different experiences, preparing to embark on a work of love for a young woman considering marriage. Intertwined—friends, sisters, daughters, grandmothers—they each contribute, and with the last stitch, a balanced and harmonious design tells the story of their lives.

The quilt "Where Love Resides," on page 52, contains blocks that represent each quiltmaker's unique declaration of love. In every block, we feel the emotional stirrings of a common bond. Like the warmth of being wrapped in a quilt, security and comfort can be found in surrounding ourselves with the people and places that enrich our lives.

Where Love Resides is a sampler of the infinite sources of love.

Passion engages body and soul and rejuvenates the spirit;

Creativity transcends the present and transforms the world;

Dreams fuel existence through the mundane moments;

Home holds the pleasures of life and belonging;

Nature invigorates through beauty, serenity, and the renewal of changing seasons;

Community enriches life through belonging and familiarity;

Mothers are the source of selfless nurturing;

Sisters offer the bond of a lifetime ally;

Lovers inspire us to bare our souls and commit our lives.

The list is not all-inclusive. The sources of love in our lives are uniquely individual. Their value lends meaning to our sojourn.

Bound together by a common passion, the employees of That Patchwork Place have dedicated the past two decades to publishing America's Best-Loved Quilt Books™, hundreds of titles by accomplished quilters, written to inspire those who share a love of fabrics, handwork, and history. Sometimes an heirloom, sometimes a whimsical piece, each quilt enhances the life of the creator and the recipient. Therefore, we feel honored to share the reflections in *Where Love Resides* with not only quilters and those who have read the novel or seen the film *How to Make an American Quilt*, but with everyone who loves.

As you read this book, you may find yourself encouraged to begin the personal journey of creating a stitched expression of love. For this reason, we have included a short section on making a quilt block. Thousands of easy-to-follow patterns are available for creating beautiful quilts. There is no pre-scribed pattern for finding where love resides. How we do this depends on the unique blueprint of our souls.

Turn the pages and reflect on the love in your life. Feel free to write personal notes on the pages and to return to this book often. Express your love by sharing *Where Love Resides* with others. It is through sharing, the overlapping of our lives, that we find the place where love resides.

Love Resides In *Sisterhood*

SISTERHOOD

A sister sits on the honored throne as a lifetime ally. By birth or shared experience, sisters are more than best friends.

In the presence of a sister, you enter the warm, soothing zone of familiarity. You confirm each other's memories and accept each other's weaknesses. A betrayed confidence, a misunderstanding, a forgotten loan,

Often a quilt is made up of what you would normally throw out — hand-me-downs, scraps, clothes that sisters shared.

an inappropriate flirtation can all mean temporary upheaval. But nothing can destroy the sacred bond between sisters.

Sisters provide support in times of crisis, share personal celebrations, and are partners in indulgence of all kinds. And in the aftermath, there is comfort in knowing she will always be on your side.

"*I think the worst part about being a woman is having women friends.*"

"*No, I think the worst part about being a woman is that you can't just be friends with a man.*"

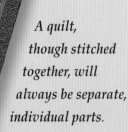

A quilt, though stitched together, will always be separate, individual parts.

We are sisters.
Linked by birth or by choice, sharing
ancestors or sharing pasts.
We offer strength, support, and healing,
Protection and understanding.
We share laughter and tears.

We are adversaries; we are conspirators.
We argue, scold, advise, and compete.
We defend, soothe, encourage, and provide.

We hurt each other, the wounds
terrible from betraying our trust.
We console each other, the solace uniquely
profound and complete.
We reveal ourselves in ways we
cannot to others.

Together we feel invincible and vulnerable,
the connection strong and gentle.
Pieced of the same fabric, held
together by the same fiber.
Fashioned from glorious opposites,
cherishing the contrast in texture.
We are sisters.

Sisters

Sisters know that
chocolate heals a
broken heart.

11

Love Resides In
The Home

HOME

Home provides the setting for life's most intense emotions. Once you enter the door, the world is behind you and the pleasures of life surround you.

Home is where memories and possessions become one. Laughter shared and tears consoled are instantly recalled with the hum of the furnace and the smells from the kitchen. Secret places and hidden emotions are all

Never underestimate the importance of your borders and your sashing. Their function is to keep the blocks apart while binding them together.

safely tucked away within reach. Every object speaks your personality, and all the truly important people in your life have shared this sanctuary.

Love is the single ingredient that transforms your dwelling into a home. Whether a bustling hive of family activity or a quiet place where you can curl up with a book, it is here that you always belong.

"There is beauty all around
When there's love at home."

JOHN HUGH MCNAUGHTON

*Study the colors
of the blocks. The right
sashing will enhance them,
bring out the best in them.
The wrong sashing will dull
them, hide their beauty.*

NO MATTER WHETHER IT IS A BEACH HOUSE, A CABIN,
A COTTAGE, A CONDOMINIUM, OR AN APARTMENT—IT IS A
RESPITE FROM THE DAY-TO-DAY MUNDANE THINGS OF LIFE.

14

Home

Home is where the heart is. Indeed, home reflects who we are and what matters to us. Walls and tabletops display family photos, offering anyone who glances a peek at the past. A collection of beautiful teapots or charming folk pieces may be irreplaceable, but we still want to use them. So it is with quilts. They add joy, warmth, and color to any room regardless of the decorating theme. Quilts, like homes, are to be used and cherished every day.

LOVE RESIDES IN FOLLOWING

Your Dreams

DREAMS

Dreams fuel human existence through the predictable patterns of life. Climb a mountain, design a home, write a book… Your aspirations are uniquely one with your soul.

Believe in yourself and begin the journey of becoming. Recapture the optimism of childhood. See yourself planting and nurturing a beautiful garden. Hear your artfully composed,

…you find the designing and creation of the quilt theme exhilarating. As if you are talking beauty with your hands.

flawlessly performed piano concerto. Taste the salt as your body glides through the warm sea.

Goethe advised, "Whatever you can do or dream you can, begin it. Boldness has genius, power, and magic in it." Immune from the judgment of others, your dreams are yours to achieve. In a world of compromises, living your dream is sublime.

Wouldn't it be nice if we could all just follow our heart's desires?

"Let's go around the world together . . . I'll study rocks while you can swim down to the bottom of canyons, swim across the middle of old volcanoes . . ."

If you have faith as a mustard seed

you shall say to this mountain,

"Move from here to there," and

it shall move; and nothing shall

be impossible to you.

MATTHEW 17:20

I've dreamt in my life dreams that have stayed with me ever after, and changed my ideas: they've gone through and through me, like wine through water, and altered the color of my mind.

EMILY BRONTË

Dreams

LOVE RESIDES IN *Motherhood*

MOTHERHOOD

Children give you purpose, new dreams, a reason for becoming a better person. The moment you are entrusted with a child, you willingly enter the ranks of the unselfish. And in this, you share a kinship with all mothers. To this young soul, you are the source of all that matters most—food, shelter, self-esteem, and love.

Your patience may be challenged

Take special care when arranging your blocks; be sympathetic to harmonies of color, fabric, and form.

and your finances depleted. On quiet nights when you peek in their rooms, you may be met with the fragrance of baby powder or unwashed gym clothes; you may face fluffy bears or posters of rock stars, but amidst it all, you'll hear the quiet rhythm of their breathing. Your eyes fill with tears and your heart with gratitude for the greatest gift of all—that of a child.

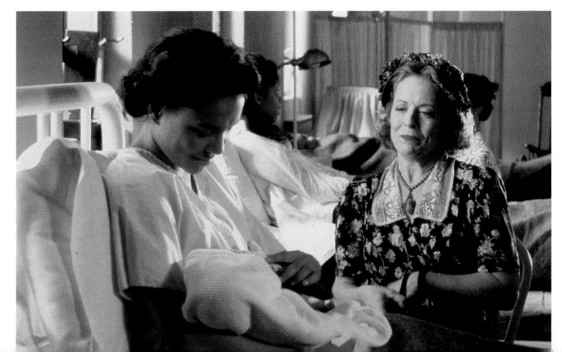

A *mother's arms are made*
of tenderness and children
sleep soundly in them.

VICTOR HUGO

"*I was not meant to find the love of a husband, but the love of a child.*"

"…*when I graft roses I take a branch from one plant and bind it to another.*  *And after they grow into each other, they become a third plant which is the best of both.*"

❋   ❋   ❋

Children

LOVE RESIDES IN
Nature

NATURE

Spring is the time of new beginnings. It is a chance to take a look at love and life with the fresh perspective of a child.

Summer, as hot and intense as adolescent emotions, provides an incubation period for exploring and maturing.

The changing leaves and bounteous harvest of autumn mark the productivity of adulthood. Now is the time for becoming, accomplishing, and sharing with those you love.

Winter chills the earth and sends living creatures into hibernation. Time slows for reflection and gathering around the hearth.

The seasons of life and the seasons of nature are harmonious. In each, there is joy and renewal.

There is beauty in the patterns of life. Quilt designs, textures, and colors can reflect what is found in nature.

"There's nothing like water to wear down a mountain and open up its secrets to you . . ."

The beauty of nature
Fills and nurtures my soul.

The peace and serenity of a quiet spot,
A meadow, a stream, a garden.

The touching perfection
of a simple leaf.
The glory of full bloom.
The miracle of life's cycle.

A river's power invigorates
me as I stand beside it.
The water rushes by.
I consider where it is going
and where it has been.
It connects places and cultures, offering
change and growth.

I watch the majesty of a sunset.
Complexity of colors
Changing and fading into night's rich darkness.

I sleep replenished.

Love Resides In
Creativity

CREATIVITY

Creativity is the outlet of a healthy soul. With a burst of creative energy, daily routines momentarily fade.

As a creative spirit, you are free to explore new impulses and follow unexpected paths. Indulgence in creativity rejuvenates and relaxes you. Ideas overtake you. Instantly, you're consumed with excitement, enthusiasm, and intensity. For one

Think of music as you orchestrate the shades and patterns; pretend you are a conductor in a lush symphony hall.

moment, all that you are becomes what you are expressing.

Sharing creativity is a bonding experience that ties lives together. A product of creativity sends a message that transcends the bounds of culture and class. Whether you write a poem, compose music, choreograph a dance, or paint a landscape, through creativity, the world is transformed.

Love is a canvas
furnished by Nature
and embroidered
by imagination.

VOLTAIRE

"Sometimes you have
to break the rules to
keep the work alive."

Creativity

"Self-expression heals the wounded heart."

LOVE RESIDES IN

Passion

PASSION

Passion overtakes all senses and leaves your conscious mind slave to the emotions of the heart. Once the fire is ignited, nothing is impossible, no task too great, no peak too high, no dream unobtainable.

The voyage is as pleasurable as the destination when passion is your guide. Control is tossed aside for elevating emotions as you indulge in

In quilts, as in other works of art, certain colors can suggest meaning, emotion, or symbolism. Red, for example, suggests passion.

the joys of the present and yield your reasoning mind to desire.

Optimism and the ability to passionately embrace new experiences and ideas adds dimension to life. A soul devoid of passion will wither in time, like a delicate plant deprived of sun. But intense passion, engaging mind, body, and soul, rejuvenates the human spirit.

Young lovers seek perfection.
Old lovers learn the art of sewing sh... together
and of seeing beauty in the multiplic... of patches
Young lovers seek perfection.

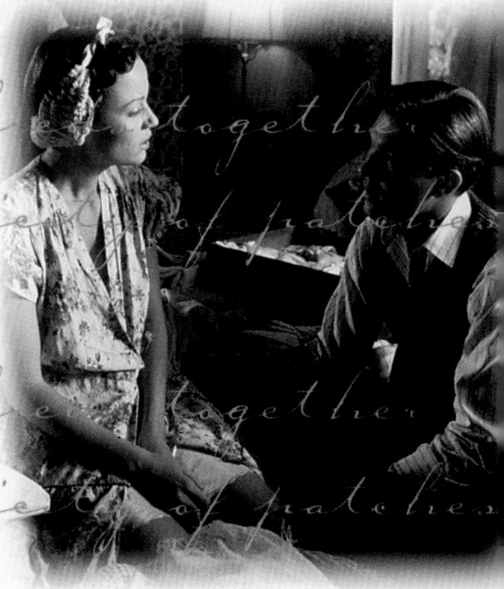

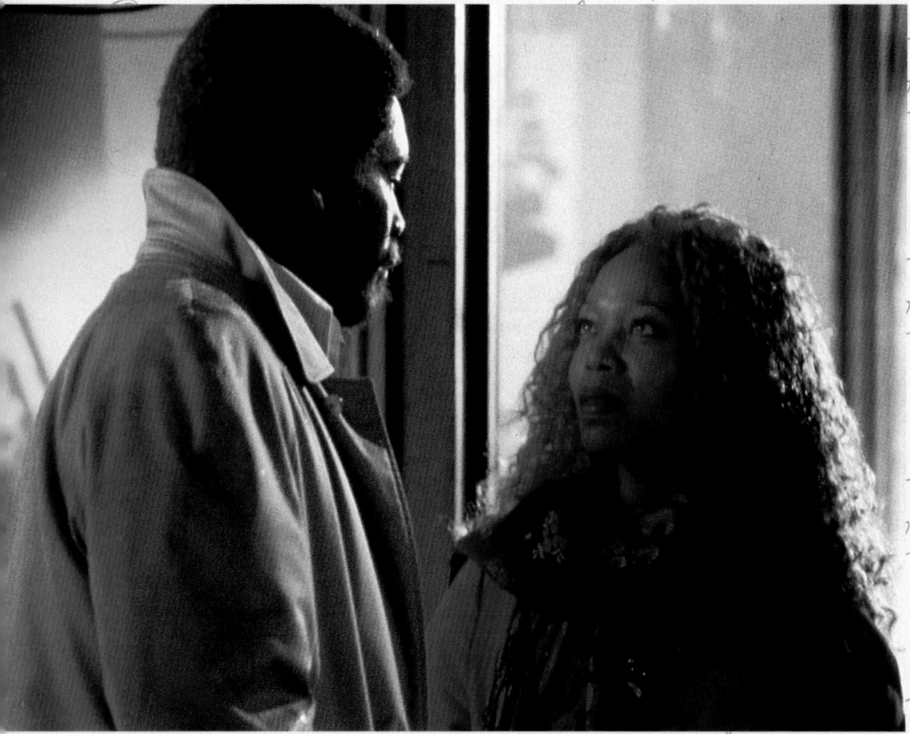

g shreds together
ltiplicity of patches

g shreds together
ltiplicity of patches

g shreds together
ltiplicity of patches

g shreds toget
and of seeing beauty in the multiplicity
Young lovers seek perfection.
Old lovers learn t
and of seeing beau

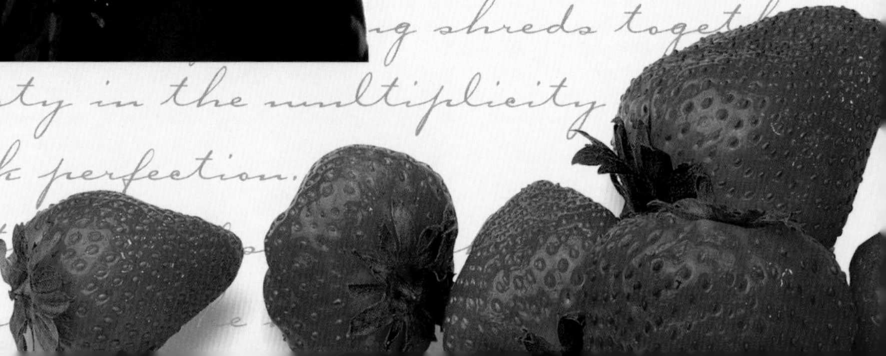

"Other thing I don't like about the moon,
it gives people an excuse to do foolish things."

Passion

When you feel passionate about something or someone, you lose all sense of time. Your mind forgets where you are and who you are. Your heart takes over with an all-consuming feeling of energy and excitement about what you're doing or who you're with. You struggle to prolong the moment, the touch, the experience, and you mourn when it is over.

Some people come across passion fleetingly in their lives, while other people fill their lives with passion for their work, their art, and their loved ones. Become passionate about something or someone and experience the feeling of caring deeply and loving intensely.

Love Resides When Souls Unite

MARRIAGE

In every heart, there is a yearning for love. The spot reserved for a soul mate is unlike any other.

Upon first meeting, you sense a spark of recognition, a surreal feeling that you are of one mind. Suddenly, your life seems interesting again, your insights fresh, your opinions valued.

When two commit in marriage as lovers and lifetime companions, the

Use only the highest-quality thread when piecing your quilt together. Remember, your intention is to make the quilt last forever.

result is an impenetrable bond. Your mate has faults, but when you are in love, the heart forgives. As a confidant, lover, and companion, your partner puts life in perspective. When you feel you've hit a dead end, your mate's presence illuminates new paths.

Your soul mate is rarely your first romance—but will always be your last love.

"I know that our marriage has as good
a chance of being wonderful as it does
of missing the mark. There is a strong
possibility that it will be both.

However, I'm banking on our love for each
other to weigh a bit heavier on the wonderful
side. I don't expect to be wrong about this.
It's a matter of faith."

In Times of Happiness

"If you had to make
the choice between
marrying a lover
or a friend, who
would you choose?"

"I would marry
my soul mate."

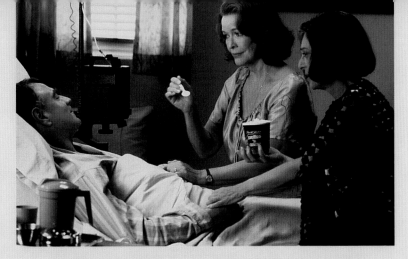

"When you've spent your life with someone and they start
to die and you feel that terrible, terrible severing, you
do things without thinking because what you
must face is so deeply unthinkable…"

And in Times of Sorrow

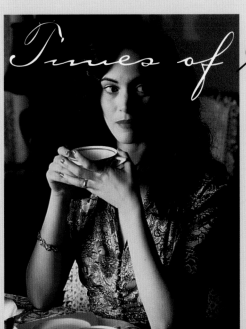

"The secret of
our marriage
is that we never
ask what the
secret is."

LOVE RESIDES IN
Community

COMMUNITY

We all have a desire to connect. Our comfort is enhanced by those who lend continuity to our lives—the grocery clerk, the school teacher, the pastor, the mail carrier. We find a sense of belonging in the ordinary, the little happenings, and the passing acquaintances. Interdependent, we consciously and unconsciously touch lives. Our

Harmonizing the different elements of the quilt is a way of creating a kind of continuity in the piece.

membership in this diverse group gives us solace.

Familiar contacts enrich our lives, and we miss them when they move on. Our experiences reveal that the strength of community can be found all around us. Indeed, community, friends, and acquaintances are the threads that tie our lives together.

Community

For as long as I can remember, my grandmother and her friends have been a part of a quilting bee.

I remember sitting under the quilting frame and pretending that I was surrounded by a forest of friendly trees . . .

. . . and that their stitches were messages from giants written across the sky.

That summer, the Grasse Quilting Bee did something they had never done before.

Anna decided that the quilt was incomplete. Constance's square had been rejected; Marianna, in protest, quit and took hers away; and Em's was missing because she said she couldn't finish it.

As Anna said . . . damn thing has no balance.

So Anna called all the quilters back and wouldn't let them go home until they got it right.

They all worked seventy-three straight hours, sustained by Anna's will and many gallons of iced tea.

The Life Before

STORY QUILTS

Story, or narrative, quilts are created to tell a story in fabric. The story can be about a quiltmaker's family member, a memory of a favorite vacation, or it can be the quiltmaker's commentary on a current news event. The story quilt on the opposite page and its story below are from the movie *How to Make an American Quilt*.

"My Aunt Pauline passed this quilt on to me. It was made by my great-great-grandmother. She called it, 'The Life Before.' It's a story quilt. It's meant to be read.

"...the creation of the world...Adam being a fool with Eve...my family's homeland...them being taken away... those are your great-great-grandparents. A crow flew over them on their wedding day...

"...a crow means either a beginning or an end. In this case it was the end. Next day, your great-great-grandfather was sold off to another farm and your great-great-grandmother never saw him again. But she had a child who was your great-grandmother. And when she was grown, slavery was ended and she was able to travel where she pleased.

"So your great-grandmother went from farm to farm trying to find her father which was a near-impossible task because Negroes at that time were left to scatter in the wind...

"One day, after many months of travel, she saw a crow sitting on a fence. And something told her to follow that bird.

"And she saw a young man working on his acre.

"And she knew in her heart that she was meant to stop right there. It seemed that the search for her father led her to a different man.

"...the man that God had intended her to marry."

Baby Quilt

CRIB QUILTS

When a woman announces that she is expecting a baby, her quiltmaking friends often leap into action and make a crib quilt for the child. Frequently, a crib quilt becomes a child's most precious possession. Not only do babies cuddle under the protective warmth of the quilt, but they become fascinated with its patterns and colors.

Many crib quilts are made from traditional patterns, such as Sunbonnet Sue or Tumbling Blocks. Appliquéd animals often adorn these quilts; other quilts feature blocks that tell stories.

Such a quilt triggers a child's imagination, opening the door to many hours of pleasure. It provides memories of comfort and security that accompany the child into adulthood. The loving thoughts that the quiltmaker stitched into the quilt are with the child for a lifetime.

The Crazy Quilt

CRAZY QUILTS

Antique Crazy quilts were most often made from scraps of silks, satins, and velvets. Even leftovers from a child's coat or a lady's favorite frock found their way into these colorful quilts. Many of them include bits of political campaign ribbons, silk cigar wrappers, and souvenir ribbons.

These fanciful quilts were embellished with embroidery stitches, showing off the maker's exceptional needlework skills. The exuberant fabrics and elegant stitches on the inside covers of this book celebrate the best of Victorian quiltmaking. Study the intricate patches and stitching.

Grasse Valley Quilt

FRIENDSHIP QUILTS

Since the mid-1700s, American women have gathered to socialize and to make quilts. Whether they worked on projects independently or collaboratively, the friendship and sharing bound them together and helped offset the hardships in their lives.

Today, groups of quiltmakers meet to share ideas, hear guest speakers, and attend workshops. Many of these groups also pool their creative talents to make quilts for needy children and families.

Popular among smaller groups of quilters are Round Robin quilts. Following guidelines or rules established by the group, each member begins a quilt, then passes it along to another member of the group. The second person adds a design or border to the quilt, then passes the quilt along to the next member, and so on. The quilt grows in size and becomes more elaborate with each turn. Eventually, each quilt is passed back to its originator, and all participants have their own wonderful, distinctive quilt, lovingly made by their friends.

No matter what kind of structure a quilt group takes, the quilters' lives are richer for their shared friendship and experiences. Friendship and quilts truly go together.

SAY IT WITH YOUR HANDS

Where does love reside for you?

Love results from and resides in the process of connection, the evolution of spirit, the bonding of person to person.

Women who quilt share their lives in many ways, seeing each other through joys, transitions, and losses, deepening their understanding of one another. Gradually, they find their way to the quilting frame, creating works of beauty while their hands work the needles, thread, and fabric. By designing images and including bits of cloth from their past, they stitch lifetimes into their quilts.

Creating offers opportunities for contemplation, reflection, catharsis, and completion. It provides a way to express something that may be difficult to say in words. Creating may be a risk or it may replace the risk of communicating in other ways.

Let the quilt "Where Love Resides" inspire you and give you gentle encouragement to create your own stories, your own memories, your own connections. One of the ways to do this is to tell a story in fabric. The section that follows includes basic instructions for making an appliqué block. Create several blocks to make an entire quilt.

Through your work, explore life's processes. Feel the flow of creativity within. Let it mirror where love resides for you.

Make a
Quilt Block

To make a quilt block that tells the story of where love resides for you, start by sketching your design. You can make one block and finish it as a single-block quilt, or if you are particularly inspired, design and make multiple blocks. Refer to the glossary, beginning on page 59.

Appliqué Basics

MAKING
APPLIQUÉ TEMPLATES

Templates for piecing include seam allowances. Templates for appliqué *do not* include seam allowances. Make templates, using cardboard or stiff paper, such as a file folder, or template plastic.

To make templates from cardboard, lay a piece of tracing paper over your design and trace the design with a sharp pencil or fine-tip permanent pen, then glue the entire page onto a piece of cardboard. Cut out the traced shapes.

To make templates from template plastic, trace the pattern pieces onto the plastic with a sharp pencil or fine-tip permanent pen, then cut out the shapes.

CUTTING THE
APPLIQUÉS

Place the template face up on the right side of the fabric. Trace around the template with a lead or chalk pencil. The drawn line marks the turned-under stitching edge. Cut out the pieces, adding a ⅛"- to ¼"-wide seam allowance all around.

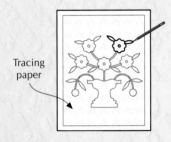

Tracing paper

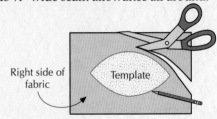

Right side of fabric

Template

CUTTING THE BACKGROUND PIECES

Carefully cut the pieces for the background blocks. The blocks for "Where Love Resides" are 15" x 15" when finished. Cut your fabric squares or pieces 1½" to 2" larger than the desired size of the finished block. This allows for the "drawing up" of the fabric during appliqué. After completing the appliqué, trim the blocks to the desired size, leaving ¼" all around for seam allowances.

THREAD AND NEEDLES

Most quiltmakers favor 100% cotton or cotton-wrapped polyester thread. It comes in a variety of colors, making it easy to match thread to fabric colors. Choose thread that matches the color of the piece you are appliquéing, rather than the background fabric.

Two types of needles are used for appliqué: Sharps and Betweens. Sharps are favored by many quiltmakers for appliquéing. Choose a needle length that is comfortable for you.

NEEDLE-TURN APPLIQUÉ

There are many techniques for appliqué; however, needle-turn appliqué is probably the most popular.

1. Pin or baste the appliqué piece to the background block.

2. Tie a knot in a single strand of thread that is approximately 18" long.

3. Start at the straightest edge of the appliqué, for example, the right side of the leaf.

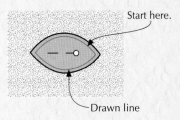
Start here.

Drawn line

4. To create a turned edge, roll the seam allowance under to the drawn line so that the line is hidden. Hold the turned portion in place with your thumb.

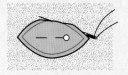

5. Work from right to left if you are right-handed, or from left to right if you are left-handed. Start on the back side of the background fabric. Bring the needle up through the background fabric and into the appliqué piece, catching two or three threads of its turned edge.

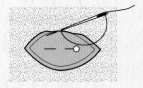

6. Insert the needle tip into the background fabric next to the point where the thread came out of the appliqué piece. Move the needle ahead ⅛", then bring it up through the background fabric and catch just two or three threads of the appliqué piece's turned edge. Make your stitches as small and invisible as possible.

7. Continue until you have stitched all around the appliqué. To end stitching, turn the block over. On the back side, take two small stitches on top of each other at the end of the just-completed stitches. From the back side, your stitches should look like small diagonal lines outlining the shape of the appliquéd piece.

Finishing the Quilt

For techniques on finishing your quilt, refer to *The Quilters' Companion: Everything You Need to Know to Make Beautiful Quilts*, compiled by That Patchwork Place. See "Suggested Reading" on page 61.

MARKING THE QUILTING DESIGN

Press your quilt top or block. Mark the quilting design on the quilt top before layering the quilt. Use stencils to mark repeated designs. Marking pens and pencils are available in a variety of colors. Always draw the lines lightly and test markers on a scrap of fabric to make sure the lines can be removed.

If you plan to quilt a design that outlines the appliqué or pieced designs in the blocks, it is not necessary to mark the design with a marker.

LAYERING THE QUILT

Fabric for the quilt back should be compatible with your quilt top. Make the backing at least 2" larger than the quilt top on all sides.

It is always a good idea to unroll the batting and let it relax overnight before you layer your quilt. After the batting has relaxed, cut it the same size as the backing.

1. Spread the backing, wrong side up, on a flat surface. Anchor it with pins or masking tape. Be careful not to stretch the backing out of shape.

2. Spread the batting over the backing, smoothing out any wrinkles.

3. Place the pressed quilt top, right side up, on top of the batting. Smooth out any wrinkles and make sure the edges of the quilt top are parallel to the edges of the backing.

4. Starting in the center, baste (long running stitches) with needle and thread and work diagonally to each corner. Continue basting in a grid of horizontal and vertical lines 6" to 8" apart. Finish by basting around the edges.

HAND QUILTING

For many quilters, hand quilting not only adds dimension to a quilt, but the process is very relaxing. The quilting stitch is actually a running stitch, made with small stitches of even lengths. All you need are short quilting needles, quilting thread, and a thimble. Most quilters use a hoop or frame to support the quilt while they work.

1. Thread the needle with a single strand of quilting thread, about 18" long. Make a small, single knot at the end of the thread. Insert the needle

through the quilt top and batting about 1" from where you want to begin quilting. Bury the knot in the batting by pulling gently until the knot pops through the top layer.

2. Take a tiny backstitch, then continue stitching along the marked stitching line. Occasionally, check to make sure your stitches go through all three layers of the quilt.

3. To end a line of quilting, make a small knot close to the last stitch. Backstitch, running the thread a needle's length through the batting. Gently pull the thread until the knot pops into the batting; clip the thread at the surface of the quilt.

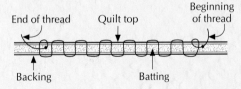

BINDING YOUR QUILT

Binding encases the raw edges of your quilt and is the final step in completing it. You can purchase bias binding or make your own. You can experience a sense of accomplishment and feel a sense of joy when you "say it with your hands."

Quilt Conservation and Care

When displaying quilts, it is a good idea to keep a few things in mind to help preserve them. Because strong light can weaken fibers and fade colors, place quilts where they will not be exposed to strong sunlight or direct artificial light. Stitch a sleeve on the back of the quilt, then hang it from a quilt display rack or from a brass curtain rod. Display systems like these do not cause excessive strain on the quilt fibers.

If you want to display your quilt on a table, cupboard, or door, be sure the surfaces are clean and free of harmful cleaning agents. Line the surfaces with a piece of muslin or acid-free tissue before placing quilts on them. Protect quilts draped on tables with a piece of glass, Plexiglas, or plastic.

People usually want to fold quilts in halves and quarters. This causes stong creases to form. Instead, make it a habit to fold all quilts in thirds, with the right side on the inside. Do not store quilts in plastic bags, because plastic does not breathe and the quilt will deteriorate over time. Instead, store them in 100%-fabric pillowcases. Quilts may be rolled around a tube that has been covered with muslin or acid-free tissue if storage space allows.

Be sure to air quilts periodically by hanging them from a clothesline and allowing them to flap in the breeze on a clear day. Avoid exposing them to direct sun. To remove dust from newly made quilts without washing, tumble them in the dryer on the "air only" cycle.

Avoid laundering quilts until it is absolutely necessary. It is best not to launder or dry-clean antique quilts. If you must launder a quilt, ask for and use cleaning products found in most quilt shops. Follow the manufacturer's directions. With proper conservation and care, your quilts can be family treasures for generations to come.

GLOSSARY OF QUILTING TERMS

APPLIQUÉ BLOCK

A design made by stitching shapes of fabric to the surface of another piece of fabric (background fabric). Curved pieces and intricate designs can easily be accomplished using appliqué techniques.

BACKING

A large piece of fabric that covers the back of a quilt. More than one piece of fabric may be sewn together to make one large piece.

BATTING

A layer sandwiched between the quilt top and the backing. Batting is available in various thicknesses and fiber content. A thick or high-loft batting is a good choice for a puffy bed quilt. A lightweight batting is ideal for wall quilts, is easier to quilt through, and gives the flat look of an antique quilt.

BINDING

A strip of fabric that is folded and sewn around the edges of the quilt to finish it.

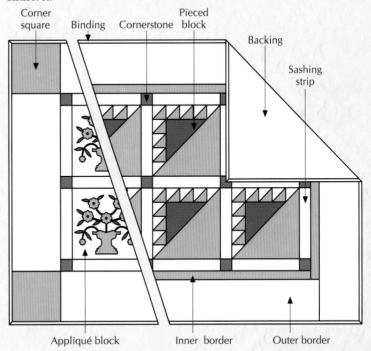

Corner square · Binding · Cornerstone · Pieced block · Backing · Sashing strip · Appliqué block · Inner border · Outer border

BORDERS

The strips of fabric surrounding the main body of the quilt top. They serve as a frame to set off the central design. Single or multiple borders of varying widths may be added.

CORNERSTONE

A square of fabric used to join two sashing strips where they intersect.

CORNER SQUARE

A square of fabric used to join two border strips where they intersect.

FABRIC

Quilt shops and fabric stores have an exciting array of fabrics. Most quiltmakers use 100% cotton fabrics, although there is growing interest in using wool, silk, velvet, and other fibers. Others assemble fabric scraps that bring to mind special memories. Quilters love to collect fabrics so that when inspiration strikes, they have a selection from which to choose.

PATTERN

A design that is usually repeated on the quilt top.

PIECING/PIECED BLOCK

Pieces of fabric sewn together to form a pattern or block. Piecing is a good way to make geometric designs or designs that contain many straight lines.

QUILTING

Short running stitches made with a single thread that goes through all three layers of the quilt—the quilt top, batting, and backing. Quilting prevents the batting from shifting.

SASHING

Strips of fabric sewn between the blocks and between rows of blocks.

SETTING (STRAIGHT AND ON-POINT)

The arrangement in which blocks are sewn together. In a straight set, blocks are laid out in rows parallel to the edges; sashing can be included. In a on-point set, blocks are laid out in diagonal rows, with triangles added to complete the sides and corners of the quilt.

TYING

A quick, alternate method of securing the three layers of the quilt together.

SUGGESTED READING

BOOKS PUBLISHED BY
THAT PATCHWORK PLACE
(1-800-426-3126)

Appliqué in Bloom by Gabrielle Swain
Appliqué Borders by Jeana Kimball
Baltimore Bouquets by Mimi Dietrich
Biblical Blocks by Rosemary Makhan
Botanical Wreaths by Laura M. Reinstatler
The Easy Art of Appliqué
    by Mimi Dietrich & Roxi Eppler
Easy Machine Paper Piecing
    by Carol Doak
The Joy of Quilting
    by Joan Hanson & Mary Hickey
Little Quilts by Alice Berg, Sylvia Johnson &
    Mary Ellen Von Holt
Machine Quilting Made Easy
    by Maurine Noble
Make Room for Quilts by Nancy J. Martin
Our Pieceful Village by Lynn Rice
Quilts from the Smithsonian
    by Mimi Dietrich
Quilted Landscapes by Joan Blalock
The Quilters' Companion
    (compiled by That Patchwork Place)
Quilting Makes the Quilt by Lee Cleland
Round Robin Quilts
    by Pat Magaret & Donna Slusser
ScrapMania by Sally Schneider
Sunbonnet Sue All Through the Year
    by Sue Linker

Watercolor Impressions by Pat Magaret &
    Donna Slusser
WOW! Wool-On-Wool Folk Art Quilts by Janet
    Carija Brandt

Quilting titles are available at quilt, craft, and bookstores. Call 1-800-426-3126 for the name of the quilt shop nearest you.

OTHER PUBLICATIONS

Otto, Whitney. *How to Make An American Quilt*. New York: Villard Books, 1991.

Otto, Whitney. *Now You See Her*. New York: Ballantine Books, 1995.

Lyons, Mary E. *Stitching Stars: The Story Quilts of Harriet Powers*. New York: Charles Scribner's Sons, 1993.

Mashuta, Mary. *Story Quilts: Telling Your Tale in Fabric*. Lafayette, Calif.: C&T Publishing, 1992.

Wahlman, Maude Southwell. *Signs and Symbols: African Images in African-American Quilts*. New York: Studio Books, in association with Museum of American Folk Art, 1993.

Look for a book of instructions for all five quilts from the film *How to Make an American Quilt*—coming in Spring 1996!

ADDITIONAL CREDITS

(continued from copyright page)

From the screenplay *How to Make an American Quilt*™ by Jane Anderson (Universal City Studios, Inc. and Amblin Entertainment, Inc. All Rights Reserved, 1995):

p. 9, "Often a quilt . . ."
p. 10, "You may not . . ."
p. 10, "I think the . . ."
p. 11, "Sisters know that . . ."
       (paraphrased)
p. 13, "Never underestimate the . . ."
p. 14, "Study the colors . . ."
p. 18, "Let's go around . . ."
p. 23, "I was not . . ." (from the movie)
p. 23, "When I graft . . ."
p. 26, "There's nothing like . . ."
p. 30, "Sometimes you have . . ."
p. 31, "Self-expression heals . . ."
p. 34, "Young lovers seek . . ."
p. 35, "Other thing I . . ."
p. 38, "I know that . . ."
p. 38, "If you had . . ."
p. 39, "When you've spent . . .
p. 41, "Harmonizing the different . . ."
p. 42, "For as long . . ."
p. 43, "That summer, the . . ."
p. 64, "What's so crazy?"

From the novel *How to Make an American Quilt* by Whitney Otto (Villard Books, a division of Random House, Inc., 1991):

p. 10, "A quilt, though . . ."
p. 15, "What you should . . ."
p. 17, "You find the . . ."

p. 18, "Wouldn't it be nice . . ."
p. 21, "Take special care . . ."
p. 29, "Think of music . . ."
p. 33, "In quilts, as . . ."
p. 37, "Use only the . . ."
p. 39, "The secret of . . ."

CONTRIBUTING WRITERS:

Introduction and chapter openers by Kathy Hoggan
p. 11, "We are sisters . . ."
       Laura M. Reinstatler
p. 14, "No matter whether . . ."
       Kerry I. Hoffman
p. 15, Kerry I. Hoffman
p. 27, "The beauty of nature . . ."
       Laura M. Reinstatler
p. 35, "When you feel . . ."
       Ursula Reikes
pp. 47, 49, 51, Kerry I. Hoffman
p. 53, "Where does love . . ."
       Laura M. Reinstatler

ADDITIONAL QUILTS:

(That Patchwork Place, Inc.)

p. 9, "Tea Party" by Mimi Dietrich © from *Tea Party Time* by Nancy J. Martin
p. 10, "Friendship Star" by Sally Schneider from *ScrapMania* by Sally Schneider
p. 13, "Jazz Cats" by Janet Kime from *The Cat's Meow* by Janet Kime
p. 14, "The Hamlet in Chantilly" by Marie-Claude Gaillochet from *Le Rouvray* by Diane de Obaldia with Marie-Christine Flocard and Cosabeth Parriaud

p. 14, from *Make Room for Quilts* by Nancy J. Martin
p. 15, from *Make Room for Quilts* by Nancy J. Martin
p. 17, "The Incredibly Cool Cosmic Rocket Ship" by Joan Hanson from *The Joy of Quilting* by Joan Hanson and Mary Hickey
p. 25, "Hummingbird" by Margaret Rolfe from *Go Wild with Quilts* by Margaret Rolfe
p. 25, "Sunset" by Joan Blalock from *Quilted Landscapes* by Joan Blalock
p. 29, "Flowers and Hearts" by Janet Carija Brandt from *WOW! Wool-on-Wool Folk Art Quilts* by Janet Carija Brandt
p. 31, "Rhapsody in Bloom" by Donna Ingram Slusser from *Watercolor Impressions* by Pat Maixner Magaret and Donna Ingram Slusser
p. 33, "Through the Year with Sunbonnet Sue Two" by Sue Linker from *Sunbonnet Sue All Through the Year* by Sue Linker
p. 37, "Double Wedding Ring" by Alice Kofahl from *Not Just Quilts* by Jo Parrott
p. 41, "Barrington Memories" by Sally Clark Cran from *Our Pieceful Village* by Lynn Rice
p. 41, "Old Glory" by Nancy Southerland-Holmes from *Old Glory* by Nancy Southerland-Holmes

What's so crazy?
This is life.
This is love.